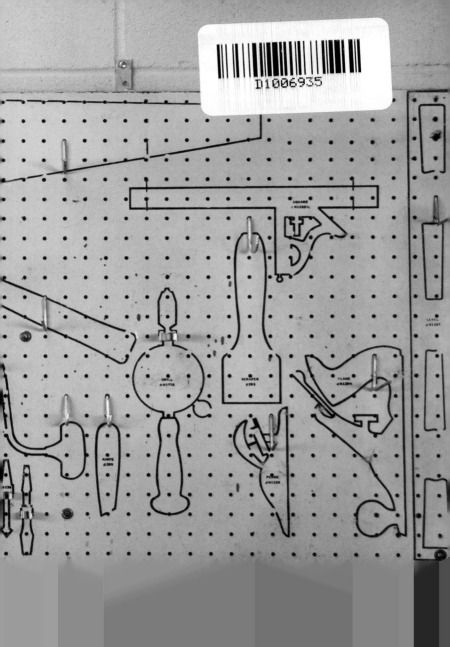

HANDS ON

HANDS ON

A MANUAL FOR GETTING THE JOB DONE

by Susan Anderson

with Carrie Snow

RUNNING PRESS
PHILADELPHIA · LONDON

ISBN 978-0-7624-5250-7
Library of Congress Control Number: 2013945762

E-book ISBN 978-0-7624-5251-4

9   8   7   6   5   4   3   2   1
Digit on the right indicates the number of this printing

Cover and interior design by Susan Van Horn
Edited by Jordana Tusman
Typography: Prohibition, Filmotype Lucky, Glypha, and Gotham

Credits for Shutterstock photography:
front cover, page 115: ©Nemeziya (sky); page 1: ©tuanyick (tape measure); page 2-3: ©Nemeziya (sky);
page 91: ©Kesu (fire); page 95: ©Rimantas Abromas (woodgrain); page 103: ©Nemeziya (sky);
pages 114, 128: ©urciser (landscape background); page 118: ©originalpunkt (fire);
pages 126-127: ©Pavel Vakhrushev (sky and landscape)

Running Press Book Publishers
2300 Chestnut Street
Philadelphia, PA 19103-4371

Visit us on the web!
www.runningpress.com

CONTENTS

INTRODUCTION

HANDS ON. Those two little words conjure the image of a can-do guy, a delicious composite of Mr. Clean, the Brawny man, and your fantasy knight in shining Armor All. While some people dream of a man who writes poetry and others swoon for the irresistible allure of a hedge fund manager, you've always been more the type to imagine—in quiet, solitary, extremely private moments—a man who really looks his best attired in a tool belt.

Just a tool belt.

Can we be frank? There's no substitute for plain old-fashioned competence. While a star of the silver screen may dazzle with brooding good looks, you just can't know how sexy he really is until you've seen him performing with a cordless drill. The singer-songwriter is so sensitive, but he only knows how to use a six-stringed axe.

That guy whose mad skills in arbitrage won the day may look good in his power suit, but can he rock your circuit box? Need we discuss the untamed animal who wins his mate under a cascade of unimpeded shower flow? It's all about the plumbing, baby. Your mother may have wanted you to marry a doctor, but what's most important is a great pair of hands and all the right tools.

This book was lovingly crafted to remind you of all the ways that a hands-on man can make your world a little better, one page at a time. This volume is a feast for your eyes and a balm for your soul; a bit of spit-and-polish for your fantasies. We can't all have a hands-on guy in our lives, but we can dream, can't we?

[CHAPTER 1]

HANDS ON

in the

BEDROOM

PROJECT #1:
WELL-HUNG

"Things getting boring in the bedroom?
A well-hung mirror will add excitement to
your décor, and make everything look bigger.
Hang the mirror so it reflects an appealing
view. Get a friend to help you find
the best position."

FINDING A STUD

POP QUIZ

A big stud is what you'll want to find to hang your mirror. How do you find a stud?

[A] In the parking lot of Home Depot

[B] By purchasing an expensive gadget, e.g., "stud finder"

[C] Calling an expert to do it right

STUD: A seducer, a ladies' man; a male animal that is kept for breeding; upright posts in the framework of a wall. Oh, let's get serious. There's only one thing you want upright.

SIZE MATTERS:
There are many tools available to do any job. The key is deciding which is the best tool to use. A good rule to follow is: Match the tool size to the job.

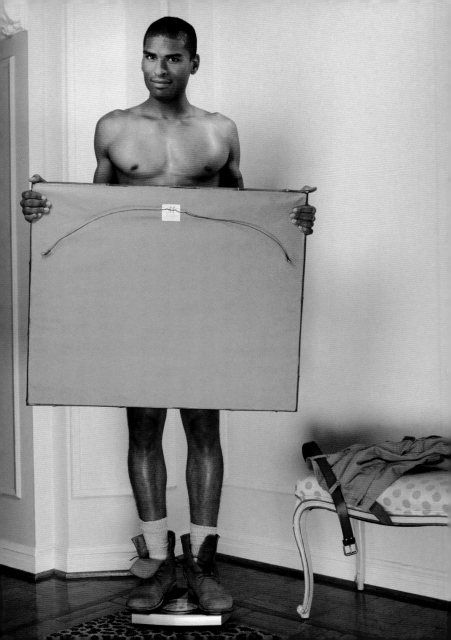

THE RIGHT HARDWARE

THE LOWDOWN: So you found your stud, but here is where size really does matter. Weigh yourself first, then step on the scale holding the mirror. Do a little math, and voilà, you can buy hardware rated to the weight of the mirror. Purchase any other gear that you might need later. Does Home Depot carry handcuffs?

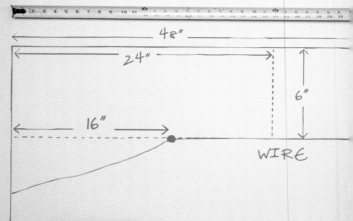

MEASURE UP

Hold your mirror up to the wall where you want to hang it, and mark the top center point of the frame. Make sure to have ample lead in your pencil. For anything really big, you're going to need a couple of hooks.

HARD FACT: Mounting without a stud can be tricky. You will need to drill a pilot hole in the wall before inserting an anchor or toggle bolt to secure a fastening base for your hardware. If you need a last-minute pilot hole, try any airport bar.

"The work you do in the bedroom always pays off in the end. It's nice to know the hard stuff is behind you. And in front of you."

PROJECT #2:

BEDROOM BUSINESS

"Personally, I like a little noise in the bedroom—
but not when it comes from a squeaky bed."

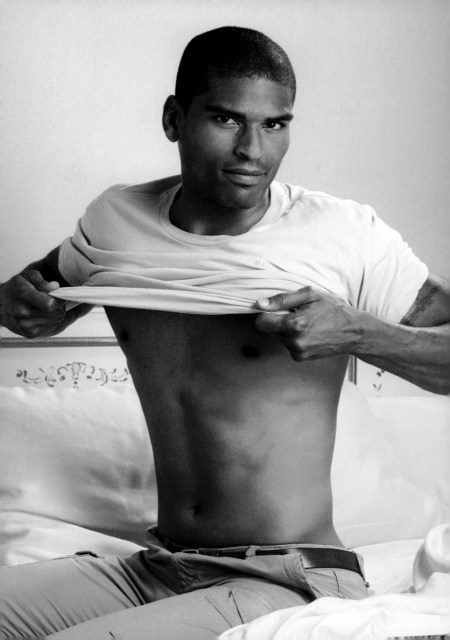

"Squeaky bedsprings are often the result of metal meeting metal or wood, unstable spring compression, or lack of lubrication. And we all know, nothing good comes from a lack of lubrication."

JUST THE TIP: Routine tightening of the nuts and bolts on your headboard or bed frame, in addition to regularly lubricating the bedsprings, is a good way to prevent the side effects of heavy use.

BANGING AND SQUEAKING

"When the headboard is banging, a doorstop screwed into the right position will protect the wall, and keep the neighbors from calling."

THE LOWDOWN: Maybe the trouble is a loose screw or problem nut. Use a wrench or screwdriver to tighten up anything that's come unhinged. Use a wench and Screwdriver to loosen up anyone else. Fresh orange juice is best.

If the springs are squeaking, a quick solution is to put something stiff between the mattress and the box spring, and not just old *Playgirl* magazines. It doesn't hurt to have something stiff on top, either.

THICK AS A BRICK

"It's great to have a Lumber Jack in bed, but not when he's sawing wood."

HARD FACT: Elevate the head of the bed by 4 to 6 inches by placing bricks under the bedposts. Elevating the torso boosts circulation, improves stamina, and may eliminate snoring.

MATTRESS DRILL

JUST THE TIP: When you turn your clocks back, rotate your mattress. Flip it in fall, and spin it in spring. I got your daylight savings right here.

STRIP, FLUFF, BEAT, AND FLIP

[1] Remove all bedding.

[2] Gently vacuum between the tufted areas, using a long, hard attachment. Make Hoover proud.

[3] Tap the mattress with a broom handle. Beat it harder to refluff large depressions. Use a plain wood-finish handle to avoid leaving marks.

[4] Keep beating the mattress for approximately 15 minutes. Or until it uses its safe word.

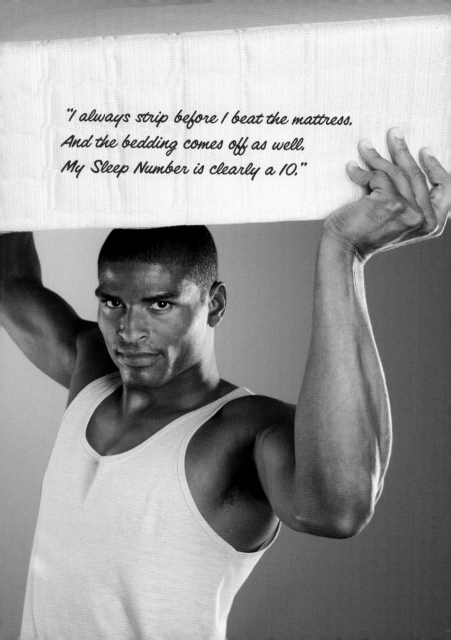

[CHAPTER 2]

HANDS ON
in the
BATH

SILICONE ENHANCEMENTS

"Silicone caulk is both a glue and a sealant used to prevent water seepage. Removing old caulk and recaulking joints between your tiles and tub will keep it snug when things get wet."

WELCOME TO THE GUN SHOW

"Don't go off half-cocked. If you have your sights set on doing the job right, find a professional tool."

HERE'S THE RUB

"Silicone caulking is a messy job, but you gotta get clean before you can get dirty. Guess where I'm hiding my caulk gun?"

JUST THE TIP:

Remove all soap scum
and grime before caulking.
How'd you get footprints that
high up?

NOT ALL CAULKS ARE ALIKE

"The competition is stiff, but there is no substitute for silicone on hard surfaces. Silicone stays soft and pliable—at least that's what the best plastic surgeons guarantee."

SEAL THE DEAL

GOOD CAULK IS EASY AS 1, 2, 3.

[1] Cut the tip at a 45-degree angle. Cut close to the tip;
     a smaller bead is easier to control.

[2] Position your caulk gun at 45 degrees to the surface.

[3] Good timing and a steady hand make for a great lay.

*"This caulk gun isn't the
only thing that's loaded
with creamy white filling."*

PIPE DREAMS

"Penetrating pipes can be hard, but with the right tool we can get to the root of the problem. The hardest-working tool isn't in this box."

TAKE THE PLUNGE

JUST THE TIP: Take the stopper out of the drain, and seal the overflow vent with duct tape.

A LITTLE BIT DEEPER: Apply a thick layer of petroleum jelly to the rim to form a tight seal.

ALL THE WAY: Push and pull. The suction is as important as the thrust.

*"Are you prepared to get wet?
Because this pipe is about to burst."*

CHEMICAL REACTION

"When you put two household staples together, it can have a volcanic effect. Just like online dating."

THE BRAZILIAN METHOD: If your problem is too much hair down there, try pouring a bottle of hair remover into the drain and wait 30 minutes. Follow with hot water.

Warning: This method to be used on clogged drains only.

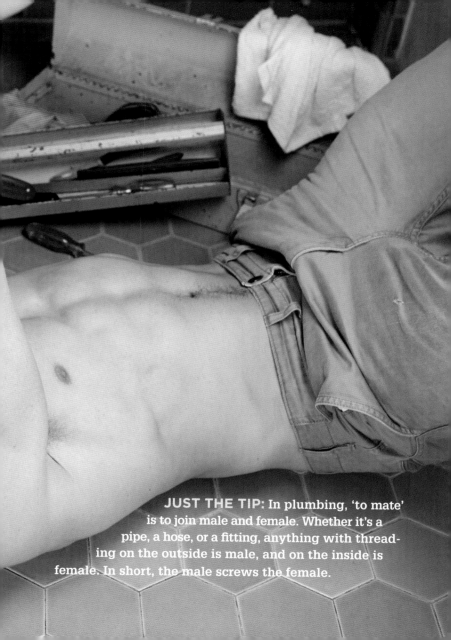

JUST THE TIP: In plumbing, 'to mate' is to join male and female. Whether it's a pipe, a hose, or a fitting, anything with threading on the outside is male, and on the inside is female. In short, the male screws the female.

WIGGLING THE SNAKE

Also known as a "toilet jack" or an "electric eel," the plumbing snake is a flexible auger used to unclog blockages that are deep within the drainpipe. It takes practice to learn how to wiggle it correctly. Call a professional.

While you are waiting for the plumber, play this word association game:

SNAKE   PIPE   HOSE   SCREW   JOINT   GUN

Hint: All the answers rhyme with Venus.

*"Does everybody have to take
their shirt off to use the phone?"*

CHAPTER 3

HANDS ON

in the

DEN

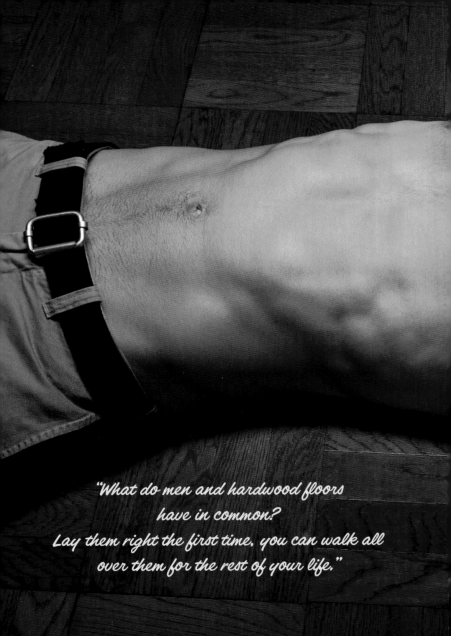

"What do men and hardwood floors
have in common?
Lay them right the first time, you can walk all
over them for the rest of your life."

PROJECT #1:

CARING FOR HARD WOOD

"Get to know your type of flooring and coating intimately. With a little care, your hardwood will serve you well. Work with the grain, and rub with gentle, even pressure until you achieve a satisfying finish. Wax on, whacks off."

LEAVE NO MARKS

"When moving furniture, lift it instead of dragging. This also applies to moving the conversation into the bedroom."

JUST THE TIP: Keep high-heeled shoes in good repair, or ask your guests to remove their shoes. Did I mention I have big feet?

DOWN ON ALL FLOORS

JUST THE TIP: Wipe scuff marks with
a damp sponge, then buff with a new
tennis ball. Your floors will love it.
But remember, to a tennis
player, love is nothing.

"Hardwood floors take a pounding. Rub them the right way, every day, and not just on the weekends."

A BUFF JOB

BUFF: A garment made of buff leather; a device having a soft absorbent surface by which polishing material is applied; having a physique enhanced by bodybuilding exercises; the state of being nude.

"You just can't beat a really good buffing. But sometimes a guy named Buffer can give you a really good beating—if you're into that."

PROJECT #2:
SHAG-WORTHY

"If your rug has been wound up tight, it's time
to unwind and spread it out. This isn't the
only thing I'm carrying that's thick."

WORKING OUT KINKS

JUST THE TIP: Place heavy items on the wrinkled portions of the rug: encyclopedias, old issues of *Cosmo*, or your three-volume set of *Fifty Shades of Grey*.

A LITTLE BIT DEEPER: Place the area rug between your mattress and box spring. For better results, add more people to the mattress.

"Bend the rug to your will. Lay it on the floor upside down, and roll it up the opposite way. Bind it securely with a rope. How long you keep it tied up is between you and your rug."

"You can also just lay out the rug in the sunlight all day. After all, who doesn't like getting laid out in the sun?"

LUNCHTIME!
An hour break will give your handyman the energy he needs for all that afternoon pounding and banging.

EXTRA PADDING

POP QUIZ

Does your rug need extra padding?

[A] Do your downstairs neighbors think you're
     studying tap?

[B] Is your life a virtual slip 'n' slide?

[C] Will a rug pad prevent rug burn?

If you answered *yes* to one or more of the above, you
need a rug pad.

SIZE MATTERS: Cut a rug pad one inch
smaller on all four sides of your rug. You don't
want your nonslip showing!

DISAPPEARING ACT

JUST THE TIP: Pour white wine on a red wine spill to neutralize the red pigment and make it easier to lift off the carpet. This means you should always have a bottle of white wine in the fridge. But you knew that already.

A LITTLE BIT DEEPER: Table salt can also be poured on the spill immediately. Dampen a cloth with club soda to lift the stain.

ALL THE WAY: For stubborn stains, combine club soda with white wine for a refreshing spritzer. Your rug will still be stained, but you won't care.

CHAPTER 4

HANDS ON

in the

KITCHEN

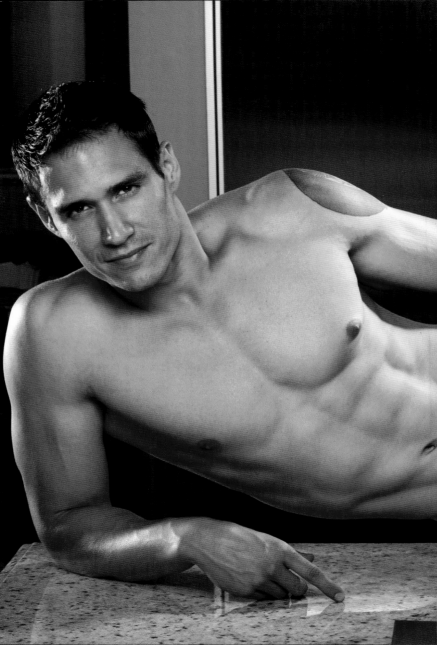

PROJECT #1:

GETTING HORIZONTAL

"Natural surfaces need special
attention. Keep them clean, waxed, and
well-oiled. They'll return the favor."

COUNTER INTELLIGENCE

Protect stone countertops from the hot items you bring home. A trivet works for pots and pans.

"What's harder than steel, smooth to the touch, and never wears out?"

HARD FACT: Formed over millions of years from compressed molten rock under the earth's surface, granite is extremely hard and durable. The only thing harder is getting him to spend the night.

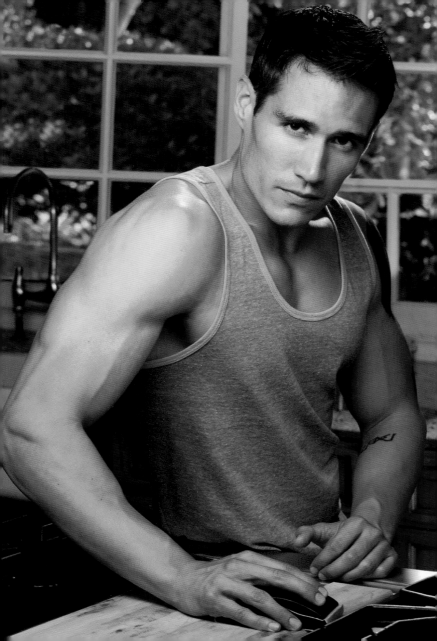

ROUTINE RUBDOWN

JUST THE TIP: Treat your butcher-block counter once a month for the first year, and once every six months after that. By "treating," we don't mean taking it to dinner and a movie.

A LITTLE BIT DEEPER: Remove stains or scratches with a sanding block, and rub liberally with mineral oil. Gives new meaning to "polishing one off."

"Rub new life into old wood.
No prescription required."

"Waxing is one of the nicest things you can do for distressed wood. It only sounds painful."

SAFE CONDUCT

"Kitchen protocol requires some simple rules
to ensure risk-free entertaining."

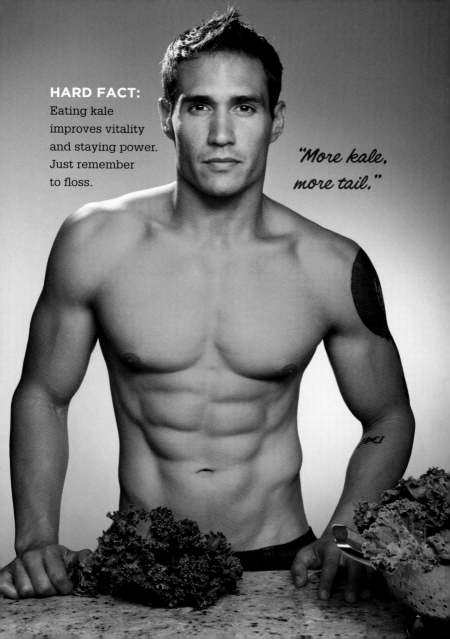

HARD FACT:
Eating kale
improves vitality
and staying power.
Just remember
to floss.

*"More kale,
more tail."*

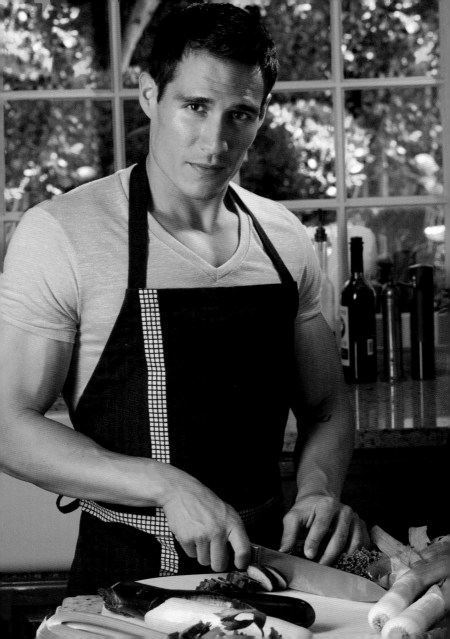

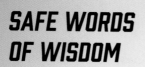

SAFE WORDS OF WISDOM

Using knives safely can extend your chef life.

"Is your blade dull and just not cutting it? A big rod helps."

THE TIP: A smoke point isn't where
...et your friends after class.

...TLE BIT DEEPER: Never pour water
...oil fire. If your pan goes up in flames,
...own the heat, and put a lid on it. Then
...our take-out menu collection.

...L THE WAY: In the event you do catch fire, stop
...ere you are, drop to the ground, and roll.
...t seriously, just try not to catch fire.

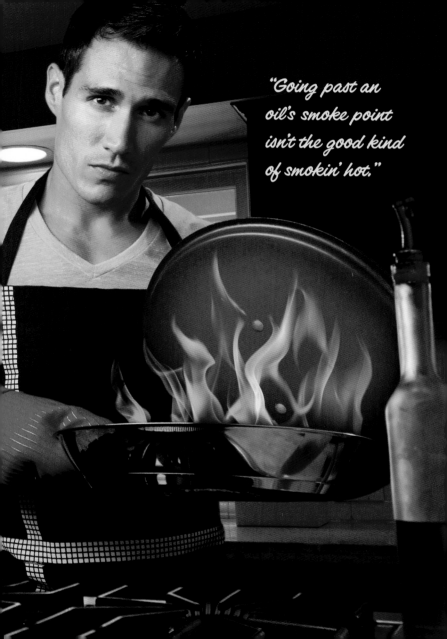

"Going past an oil's smoke point isn't the good kind of smokin' hot."

WHERE THERE'S SMOKE

Make sure to install the smoke detector a safe distance from cooking fumes and smoke. Like all of your personal entertainment devices, a smoke detector needs fresh batteries to keep it running smoothly.

"And a well-charged battery keeps you safe from calling an old boyfriend in an emergency."

"Nothing is more romantic than a candlelight dinner. And nothing is less romantic than dialing 911. Keep the heat just between you and your date."

BURN NOTICE

→ 3/4 of all sex happens in the bedroom.

→ 1/3 of all house fires are started by candles left unattended in the bedroom.

→ 1/2 of all candle fire deaths occur between midnight and 6 a.m.

As someone's mother said, "Nothing good ever happens after midnight." She was wrong, but you should definitely blow the candles first.

Making a PASS isn't always sexual.
It's also how to use a fire extinguisher.

[P] ull the pin

[A] im the nozzle

[S] queeze the lever

[S] weep from side
to side

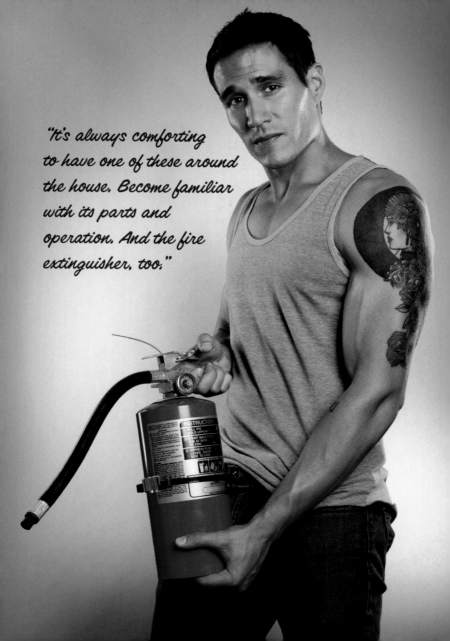

"It's always comforting to have one of these around the house. Become familiar with its parts and operation. And the fire extinguisher, too."

CHAPTER 5

HANDS ON

in the

LIVING ROOM

GETTING IN
THE MOOD

"Lighting can dramatically affect your mood.
The smallest changes can make the biggest
difference. Gosh, that sconce makes me horny."

DIM THE LIGHTS

Warm light sources, in hues from red to yellow, stimulate intimate feelings. That's why sunrises, sunsets, and candles equal romance.

"Hey, look, the sun's not the only thing up this morning."

"To create a romantic atmosphere at home, use warm-colored shades that mimic candlelight. Low light causes the pupils to dilate, which is a sign of arousal."

POSITIONING THE SWITCH

"To take matters into your own hands, install a dimmer switch. It just glides right down to sexy."

BUMP AND GRIND

*"Music can also set the right tone.
I'll put this on, you take that off?"*

music to
Strip to

all time sizzling
burlesque hits!

PROJECT #2:
TURN ON THE HEAT

*"Love is like a fire.
It can keep you warm
all night, but if you
don't watch it, it can
fizzle and leave you
in the cold."*

PRIMING THE PASSAGE

THE LOWDOWN:

[1] Open the damper. You will feel a cold draft when it's open. Like going commando.

[2] Twist two pieces of newspaper together and light the end, making a "torch."

[3] Hold the burning newspaper near the opening of the flue, and heat the damper for a few minutes.

[4] When you feel the draft reverse, the flue is primed for action.

JUST THE TIP: Before you build a fire in your fireplace, make sure the chimney is clear. A clean shaft makes for a happy log.

"Smoke should be drawn up and out the chimney. A closed flue will send smoke back into the room, putting a serious damper on the mood."

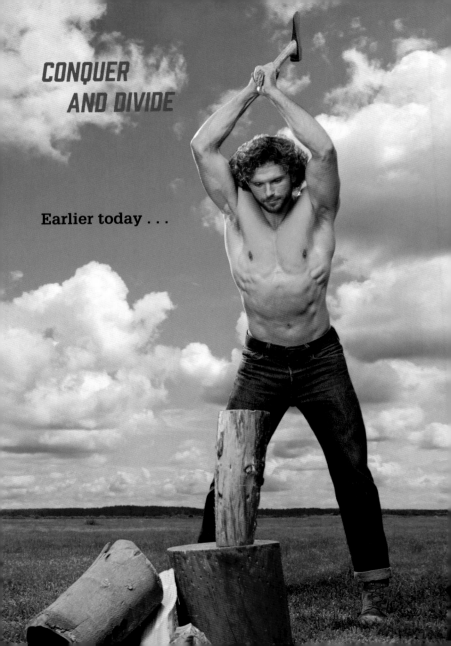

CONQUER
AND DIVIDE

Earlier today . . .

"Henry Ford said chopping your own wood warms you twice. Henry also called an assembly line a gang bang."

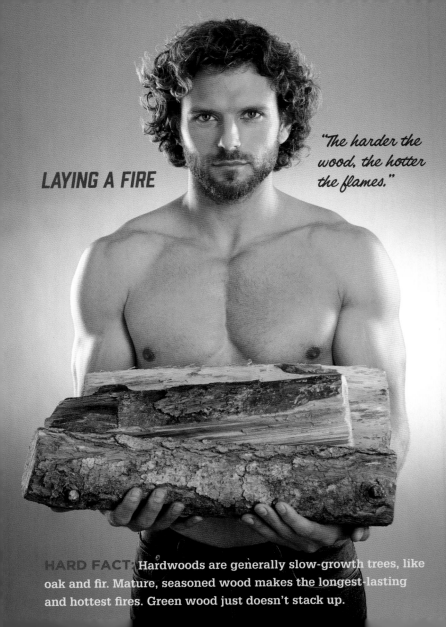

LAYING A FIRE

"The harder the wood, the hotter the flames."

HARD FACT: Hardwoods are generally slow-growth trees, like oak and fir. Mature, seasoned wood makes the longest-lasting and hottest fires. Green wood just doesn't stack up.

Newspaper

Kindling

Wood

Tired of the same old positions? Try an upside-down lay. Big logs first, then kindling, with tinder on the top. Like a reverse cowgirl, but with real fire. Screw the cookies—this is the best Girl Scout badge ever.

"Is it hot in here,

        or is it just you?"

SMOLDERING REMAINS

Don't leave a burning fire unattended. Give the fire some time to cool down. Unless you're banging Smokey the Bear.

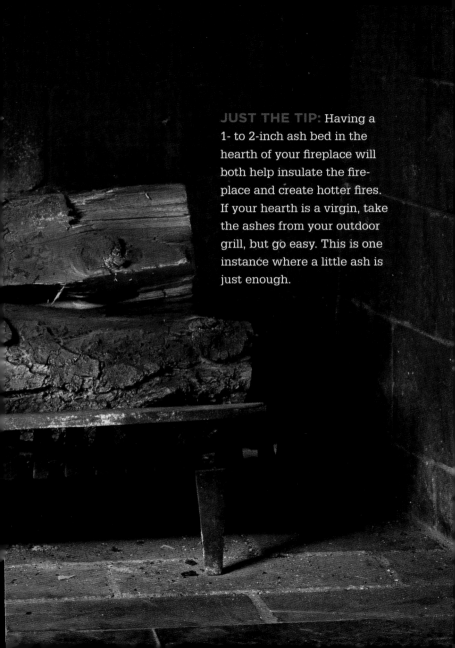

JUST THE TIP: Having a 1- to 2-inch ash bed in the hearth of your fireplace will both help insulate the fireplace and create hotter fires. If your hearth is a virgin, take the ashes from your outdoor grill, but go easy. This is one instance where a little ash is just enough.

How to Pick Your Handy Man

[1] Don't choose a handy-man solely on his looks, although they can't hurt.

[2] A good handyman has a good heart. Get a stethoscope and check under the pecs.

[3] Ask for personal references from previous clients he has serviced.

[4] Does he clean up after himself? A good handy-man doesn't leave a mess behind when the job is done.

[5] Look for clear eyes, firm skin, and strong teeth. A handyman is only as good as his last checkup. Stamina, strength, and unimpeded vascular flow depend on it.

[6] Don't give him too long a leash until you are sure that he's well-trained.

[7] Don't be afraid to ask to see a tool before any work gets underway.

[8] Take a good long look at his tools. Evidence of wear, poor maintenance, or, worst of all, a broken tool, makes a handyman useless at best and down-right dangerous at worst.

[9] Make sure your handyman understands the scope of work and the terms of the contract. You don't want the job to go on too long, or for him to take off before you're completely satisfied. And if you know you've got more work for him, be sure you get a commitment.

[10] Remember, a skilled handyman is always in demand, so don't let a good one get away!

THANKS AND ACKNOWLEDGMENTS

A book like this takes a small army to produce, from the production of the photographs to the writing of the text. I would like to first express my gratitude to everyone on the crew. Your hard work and creativity made the shoot a big success, and as they say, the proof is in the pudding—or perhaps, in the beefcake?

To the writers who helped craft the manuscript, a funny line or clever turn of phrase is no easy task, and I would like to thank the following people for their contributions: Fred Rubin and Marley Simms, for their help on the original pitch; Carrie Snow, your lines make me laugh every time I read them; Paula Killen, for helping me organize and polish the text; and to Jay Leggett for your special creativity.

A book like this is nothing without great-looking models. I would like to thank my subjects; I am certain you all spent extra hours lifting weights and doing sit-ups to prepare for the shoot, and it really shows: MicQuick, Jake Lockett, Paul Teodo, Michael Long, and Michael Lanham. Thanks to Skotti Collins, Billy Marti, and models Brian McCabe, Christian Bonello, and Kerim Troeller. Here's to Tony Napoli for helping with test shoots, and to Rick Gradone and Phoebe Dawson for grooming them. Carolyn Bannos, your skills were underutilized on this project—the guys were so good-looking, retouching was not required.

Hunky models need complementary backgrounds. Thank you Sergio, Mark, and Gary for the use of your photogenic horizontal surfaces, and to Hutchins Foster and Michael A. Sheppard for hosting our shoot at the last minute. Bryan Walsingham, thanks for entrusting me with grandfather's toolbox, and to both Mark Landres and Bryan for making "the compound" available for the original test shoots.

Thanks to all of my talented friends who generously supported this project: Michael Cioffoletti, your impeccable style is evident on every page; Alexander Irvine, your artful layouts helped to sell this concept; Annie Morse, your genius never ceases to amaze me (who knew you could write jokes?); Jeff Schoen, for photographing my dad's tool bench for the end pages; Rick Morris, for creating original album cover art; Kevin Posey, it was an honor to have you on set. Thanks also to Len Peltier and PJ of Levi's for the nice pair on our cover model, and Samson Ghaffary for the handsome tool belt.

Thanks to Running Press, and editor Jordana Tusman, for choosing this book for publication, and designer Susan Van Horn for her craft and dedication to the project. Thanks also to Karrie Witkin for believing in this concept early on.

My heartfelt thanks to Alan Harris, for always being in my corner—you are a gem. And last but not least, to my mother, Dorothy, and late father, Paul. I would like to dedicate this book to my father, who did not really know how to fix anything, but was always ready to try—you made me love photography.

CREDITS

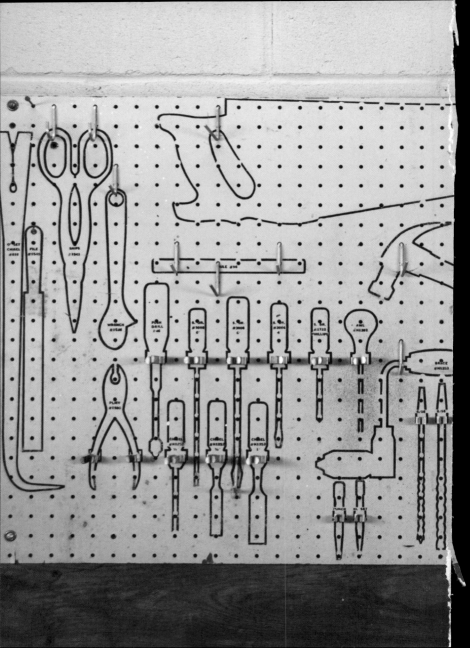